May 10, 1916

They land on the uninhabited side of South Georgia.

April 15, 1916

The crew lands on Elephant Island and sets up camp there.

August 30, 1916

Shackleton returns to Elephant Island on the Chilean Navy tugboat *Yelcho*. The entire crew is rescued.

April 24, 1916

Shackleton and five others set sail for South Georgia in the lifeboat *James Caird*.

1919

Shackleton publishes a book about the expedition, called *South*.

April 9, 1916

After months of drifting on ice floes, the crew reaches clear water and is able to launch the ship's lifeboats.

May 19–20, 1916

Shackleton and two others trek across the island to the Norwegian whaling station at Stromness.

Shackleton's Antarctic Expeditions

SIR ERNEST SHACKLETON (1874–1922) took part in four expeditions to the South Pole. The expeditions are often referred to by the names of the ships on which the explorers sailed:

1. The *Discovery* expedition (1901–1904), commanded by Robert Falcon Scott; Shackleton was third officer.

2. The *Nimrod* expedition (1907–1909), commanded by Shackleton.

3. The *Endurance* expedition (1914–1917), described in this book.

4. The *Quest* expedition (1921–1922), during which Shackleton died, on January 5, 1922.

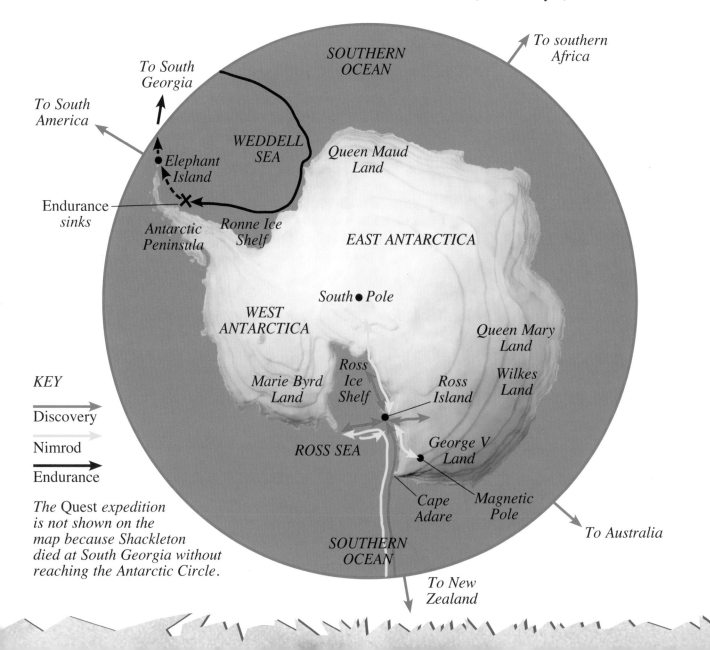

Author:

Jen Green graduated from the University of Sussex, England, with a Ph.D. in English literature in 1982. She has worked as an editor and manager in children's publishing for 15 years and is now a full-time writer. She has written many books for children.

Artist:

David Antram was born in Brighton, England, in 1958. He studied at Eastbourne College of Art and then worked in advertising for 15 years before becoming a full-time artist. He has illustrated many children's nonfiction books.

Series creator:

David Salariya was born in Dundee, Scotland. He has illustrated a wide range of books and has created and designed many new series for publishers in the UK and overseas. David established The Salariya Book Company in 1989. He lives in Brighton with his wife, illustrator Shirley Willis, and their son, Jonathan.

Editors:

Karen Barker Smith, Stephanie Cole, Stephen Haynes

Editorial Assistant: **Mark Williams**

Published in Great Britain in 2017 by
The Salariya Book Company Ltd
25 Marlborough Place, Brighton BN1 1UB

ISBN-13: 978-0-531-23832-5 (lib. bdg.) 978-0-531-23154-8 (pbk.)

All rights reserved.
Published in 2017 in the United States
by Franklin Watts
An imprint of Scholastic Inc.

A CIP catalog record for this book is available from the Library of Congress.

Printed and bound in China.
Printed on paper from sustainable sources.

1 2 3 4 5 6 7 8 9 10 R 26 25 24 23 22 21 20 19 18 17

PAPER FROM
SUSTAINABLE
FORESTS

You Wouldn't Want to Be a Polar Explorer!

Written by
Jen Green

Illustrated by
David Antram

An Expedition You'd Rather Not Go On

Created and designed by
David Salariya

Franklin Watts®
An Imprint of Scholastic Inc.

Contents

Introduction

The year is 1912. The great age of polar exploration is coming to an end. For the last four centuries, brave, hardy adventurers have been exploring the Arctic and Antarctic, the icy lands and seas in the far north and south. Sailors explored the Arctic first, looking for a new sea route that would lead to wealthy China. They never found a safe route, because Arctic waters are too icy. Then explorers discovered the huge, frozen continent of Antarctica and mapped its coast. During the early 1900s, they raced to be first to reach the North and South Poles, the most northerly and southerly points on the planet. Just three years ago, in 1909, American sailor Robert Peary finally conquered the North Pole. In 1911, Norwegian explorer Roald Amundsen just beat Captain Robert Scott of the British Navy to the South Pole.

Explorers are now racking their brains to find new challenges. Irishman Ernest Shackleton, leader of several trips to Antarctica, has dreamed up a daring plan for a new trip to the far south. You are a hardened sailor named Frank Worsley, and you volunteer to join Shackleton in what will prove to be one of the most grueling adventures of all time. You soon learn that you really wouldn't want to be a polar explorer!

A Mad Mission

Planned Antarctic crossing route

Weddell Sea

South Pole

Ross Sea

Shackleton plans to make the first overland crossing of the vast continent of Antarctica via the South Pole. That's 2,060 miles (3,330 km) across a mostly uncharted, frozen wilderness! Shackleton puts an ad in a newspaper: "Men wanted for hazardous journey. Small wages, bitter cold, long months of complete darkness, constant danger, safe return doubtful. Honor and recognition in case of success." You read the ad with great interest. Eager for adventure, you apply immediately. Shackleton decides to take you on!

THE PLAN is to set off from the Weddell Sea and cross Antarctica with a small team using sleds. On the last leg of the trip, you will use supplies left by another team setting off from the Ross Sea.

SHACKLETON'S LAST EXPEDITION was in 1909. His team nearly reached the South Pole, hauling their own sleds, but had to turn back 100 miles (160 km) away from their goal. Shackleton was knighted for his efforts — he's Sir Ernest now.

Destination Antarctica

The Endurance

By the summer of 1914, Shackleton's ship is ready. Built especially for polar travel, she is named *Endurance*, in honor of Shackleton's family motto: "By endurance we conquer." You are an experienced sailor, so Shackleton has made you captain. You organize the loading of supplies and then end up doing most of the hard work yourself! The ship's crew is a mix of tough old fishermen and polar experts, including several scientists just out of college. Also on board are sixty husky dogs to pull the sleds, two pigs to provide meat, and the ship's cat, Mrs. Chippy.

The crew

Ship and Crew:

ENDURANCE is a three-masted sailing ship that also has engines. Built with very hard wood, she is designed to ram her way through the ice in polar seas.

THE EXPEDITION includes two doctors, a cook, a carpenter, an artist, and a photographer. Officers, including an expert navigator and engineer, help you run the ship.

THE CREW of twenty-eight men ends up including a stowaway who sneaks on board when the ship docks at Buenos Aires, Argentina.

8

You set off on August 8, 1914, just as World War I begins. Heading south, you stop at Grytviken whaling station on the lonely island of South Georgia in the South Atlantic. The whalers report that the seas are very icy this year.

Stuck in the Ice

In December 1914, the ship enters the Weddell Sea. After just two days, you begin to meet large chunks of floating pack ice! You battle onward, but six weeks later, your luck runs out. Only 100 miles (160 km, about a day's sail) from land, the ship becomes firmly wedged in a great slab of ice.

In February, the ice cracks, and you see water lapping near the ship. You and the others try to dig a channel through to reach the water, but the ice is too thick. There is no radio contact with the outside world, so no one is about to rescue you. There is nothing to do but sit tight as the stricken ship drifts with the ice slowly northwest — in the wrong direction, away from land.

January

JANUARY is midsummer in Antarctica. It is light for 24 hours a day. Everyone works long hours and forgets to go to bed, so you all get very tired.

Whoosh

To prevent boredom, set up goalposts on the ice and play soccer. It's hard to keep on your feet!

July

THE MONTHS PASS, and winter arrives. In May, the sun disappears below the horizon, and for the next four months there is continual darkness. You break up the long, dark days by racing the dogs in the moonlight.

Crack!

Abandon Ship!

Months pass, and *Endurance* is still stuck fast. In August 1915, the pack ice moves and slowly begins to crush the ship. In October, loud groans and cracking sounds are heard as the hull timbers split and the glass shatters. The ship is thrown upward and suddenly lurches onto its side while you are below deck. An icy torrent pours in, and supplies, men, and dogs slide into the water! You work the pumps day and night, but it's no use. Finally, Shackleton gives the order to abandon ship, and you move onto the ice.

HELP!

SUPPLIES. In the panic, you manage to save only a few vital provisions. Three lifeboats, the sleds, navigating equipment, and the ship's banjo are piled up on the ice.

ON THE ICE. You spend your first night on the ice in a freezing tent. The temperature is -16°F (-28°C). The moon shines so brightly that it keeps you awake.

Hauling over the Ice

Your Clothing:

UNDERCLOTHES. Next to your skin, you wear long underwear and thick socks, with a pullover and trousers on top.

TOP LAYER. A windbreaker protects you from snow and howling blizzards. Your outfit is completed by a wool hat, gloves, and heavy boots.

ndurance finally sinks below the waves in November 1915, after ten months frozen in the ice. You are now marooned far out at sea. The nearest land, Paulet Island, off the tip of the Antarctic Peninsula, has a hut and supplies, but it's 400 miles (650 km) away! Shackleton decides to make for it across the ice, dragging two lifeboats.

1, 2, 3... HEAVE!

You and the rest of the crew are harnessed in teams to "manhaul" the boats, each of which weighs over a ton! In a week you make only 7 miles (11 km) headway. At this rate, it will take a year to reach land — but you have less than two months' food! Shackleton gives up and tells you to set up camp on the ice. Eventually the ice will either melt or drift near land — if you don't starve first!

Handy Hint

Gulp!

Eat the organs of freshly killed animals to avoid getting scurvy, a disease caused by lack of vitamin C.

Ice Camping

What's on the Menu?

DINNER is the same every day. It's either seal or penguin meat, if you're lucky. From the ship's stores, you managed to save only walnuts and onions — not exactly a balanced diet.

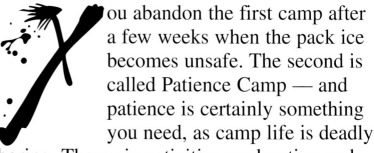

ou abandon the first camp after a few weeks when the pack ice becomes unsafe. The second is called Patience Camp — and patience is certainly something you need, as camp life is deadly boring. The main activities are hunting and trying to keep warm. You kill seals for meat and use their blubber (fat) to fuel the stove. You have to keep a careful watch for fierce leopard seals, whose huge fangs could kill you in an attack. By March 1916, the camp has drifted so far north that you reach the edge of the pack ice region.

Your Accommodation:

PASSING TIME. In warmer weather you play cards in the tents. When it's very cold, you huddle in your reindeer-skin sleeping bags, but there aren't enough bags to go around.

Handy Hint

Build ice cairns and string ropes between them to mark the edge of the camp. Now you can feel your way around in blizzards and not get lost.

You see, patience is a virtue!

Someone gag that man before I throttle him!

17

Journey to Elephant Island

The Ice Breaks Up:

ON THIN ICE. As the ice gets thinner, you can feel the swell of the waves beneath. All the bobbing up and down makes you seasick!

ON THE OCEAN WAVE. You launch the boats and sail north, rowing madly. Giant waves crash down on the boats, and salty spray soaks you to the skin.

By April 1916, the ice breaks up enough for you to launch the three lifeboats. Shackleton decides to make for Elephant Island, 100 miles (160 km) to the north. Everyone is glad to be off the ice at last, but the journey is pretty scary. The little boats weave their way between towering icebergs that threaten to crush them into matchwood. Crashing waves could swamp the boats at any moment.

I've got you, lad!

ICY BATH. In the icy water, your shipmate will last only a few minutes. Shackleton comes to the rescue and yanks him to safety — a lucky escape!

You spend the whole journey wet to the bone, freezing, and hungry. Some of your shipmates get frostbite. At night you land if there is a large slab of ice to camp on, but the thin ice is treacherous. One day, the ice splits right under the tents, and one of your shipmates falls into the water in his sleeping bag!

ONE DAY'S RATION. Your food for each day consists of one hot drink and a ship's biscuit. It doesn't get much tougher than this!

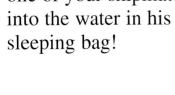

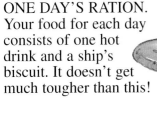

Phew! That was close!

HUNGRY KILLER WHALES leap around the boats, eyeing you for dinner. If one lands on the tow ropes that link the boats together, you'll all be dragged into the sea!

Land at Last

ELEPHANT ISLAND. The island you've reached has sheer cliffs and fresh water. There are colonies of seals and penguins (no elephants).

SAFE ON LAND. It's been 497 days since you last set foot on land! Some sailors bury their faces in the pebbles, sobbing. Others giggle hysterically.

After a week at sea, everyone cheers when Elephant Island is finally spotted. In the crashing waves, it takes three hours just to find a place to land! As the boats crunch onto the beach, you leap into the surf and claw your way onto firm ground. You try to pitch the tents on the beach, but the wind rips them to shreds. You huddle under the upturned boats and fall asleep. Whaling ships never stop at Elephant Island, and the nearest manned station is on South Georgia, hundreds of miles away — so you're not home and dry yet.

Yikes!

Z Z z

HOT FOOD! The cook has a cook-out on the beach. It's your first hot food and drink in days!

Off Again in an Open Boat

Preparing the Boat:

YOU HELP the carpenter get the boat ready for launching. You raise the boat's sides with wooden planks and nail on a canvas deck.

With no rescue likely, Shackleton decides to make for South Georgia in the strongest lifeboat. The island lies 800 miles (1,300 km) away across the world's stormiest seas. He chooses a small team to go with him. You were an expert navigator on the way to Elephant Island, so Shackleton picks you, three sailors, and the ship's carpenter.

WATERPROOFING. You seal the boat's seams with oil paint and seal blood. To keep the boat steady in high seas, you load it with 2 tons of rocks.

MEN OVERBOARD! You set off from Elephant Island on April 24, 1916. As you launch the lifeboat, waves almost capsize her, and two sailors tumble overboard. Your superstitious shipmates take this as a bad omen. The whole voyage is a long struggle to keep afloat. You spend your time working the pump and sails and bailing madly. It seems unlikely that you'll ever see the rest of the crew again.

What a start!

Handy Hint

Hmmmm

Steer the boat by using a sextant. This works by taking measurements of the position of the sun or stars. In cloudy weather, it's hard to take readings at all!

OFF DUTY. You try to sleep under the deck, lying on the rocks in a rotting reindeer-skin bag. It is so cramped that you feel like you are being buried alive!

A Speck in the Ocean

It will be a miracle if you reach South Georgia. The island is a tiny speck in a huge ocean. It is almost impossible to plot your course accurately in a small, heaving boat, and if your measurements are off by even a fraction, you'll miss the island. Howling winds could sweep you into the open ocean, and the next landfall is Africa, 4,000 miles (6,440 km) away! One night, an enormous wave bears down on the boat. You are tossed around, and a torrent of icy water almost sinks the boat, but everyone bails furiously and somehow you stay afloat. After two weeks at sea, you glimpse the black cliffs of South Georgia through the fog. You've made it! A hurricane nearly drives you onto the rocks, however, and it's another two days before you can land.

BAILING OUT. Fifty-foot (15-m) waves are common. When a big wave hits, everyone bails madly using any container he can find, as you fight to stay afloat.

YOUR RATIONS include a cup of hot soup twice a day. Salt gets into the drinking water, so everyone is very thirsty by the time you land!

SIGNS OF LAND. After fourteen wet, freezing-cold days, you spot seaweed floating on the water and then birds, which suggest that land is near at last.

Handy Hint

Keep chipping off the thick ice that forms on the rigging, or it will capsize the boat!

I've changed my mind. I want to go home.

Meanwhile...

ON ELEPHANT ISLAND. Your shipmates transform the upturned boats into a crude shelter, which they name the Snuggery. There is little room inside, and the men are packed together. They survive on a diet of limpet (a mollusk) and seaweed stew.

25

Over the Mountains

The Journey Begins:

AFTER A WEEK'S REST, three of your shipmates are too exhausted to move. You leave them resting under the upturned boat and set off by moonlight.

You spend a week on the beach on South Georgia, recovering from the journey. You've landed on the wrong side of the island, however, and the whaling station is still 150 miles (240 km) away by sea! A range of mountains lies between you and safety. Shackleton decides to make for the whaling station overland and picks you and one other sailor to go with him. You set off with a few days' rations stuffed in socks. Eventually, you discover a route through the mountains, only to find yourselves at the top of a huge snowslope as night falls. You've got to get down, or you'll freeze to death! Using a coil of rope as a makeshift toboggan, you whizz down the slope at breakneck speed and land safely in a soft bank of snow.

Follow me!

TOWERING CLIFFS, icy glaciers, and deep crevasses bar the way to the whaling station. You leap crevasses and cut steps in the ice using a carpentry tool as an ice axe. The rope tying you together is meant to keep you safe, but if one of you falls, he might pull the others down with him!

AAArrgghh!
Handy Hint
Put screws into your boot soles so that they will grip the ice better.

To the Rescue

Early next morning, you hear the toot of the whaling station whistle. Nine hours later, you stagger into the station. Your hair is long and matted, and your faces are black with grime. The first people you meet are two boys, who run away at the sight of you! The whalers welcome you and give you hot food and a comfortable bed. They rescue your shipmates on the beach and, later, you return for the men on Elephant Island. The expedition has been a disaster from start to finish, but at least it ends well!

Boat journey to South Georgia, April 24–May 10, 1916

Launch boats for Elephant Island, April 9, 1916

Elephant Island

Drift on ice floes

Endurance sinks, November 21, 1915

Endurance crushed. Ship abandoned October 27, 1915

Drift in pack ice

Hello!

Arrive Stromness
whaling station,
May 20, 1916

Depart Grytviken
whaling station,
December 5, 1914

South
Georgia

Entered pack ice,
December 7, 1914

South Orkney
Island

Heavy
pack ice

Heavy pack ice

Endurance
trapped, January
18, 1915

Help! Monsters!

Hooray!

Hurrah!

Handy
Hint

To keep their spirits up, the men
left on Elephant Island make
lists of their favorite desserts and
read aloud from a cookbook.

RESCUE. Four
months after you set
off from Elephant
Island, you return to
rescue the marooned
men. Amazingly
enough, everyone is
safe… and delighted
to see you!

ERNEST SHACKLETON
ends his days in Antarctica.
Four years after your return to
England, you head south with
him on another expedition. He
dies of a heart attack on South
Georgia and is buried there.

Glossary

Antarctic The region in the far south of Earth, surrounding the South Pole.

Arctic The region in the far north of Earth, surrounding the North Pole.

Blizzard A storm with high winds blowing powdery snow.

Blubber The layer of fat found under the skin of seals and penguins. It keeps the animals warm and can be burned to provide light and heat.

Cairn A pile of stones or ice blocks, often built to mark path routes or the summits of mountains.

Crevasse A deep crack in a glacier, sometimes hidden by snow.

Endurance The ability to withstand difficulties and stress for a long time. Also the name of Shackleton's ship.

Frostbite A condition caused by extreme cold, which destroys the tissues of the body. The ears, nose, toes, and fingers are the areas most often affected by frostbite.

Glacier A river or large mass of ice, formed by packed-down snow. The ice in a glacier flows very slowly from high ground down toward the sea.

Hazardous Extremely dangerous.

Hull The body or frame of a ship.

Husky A powerful dog used in the Arctic and Antarctic for pulling sleds.

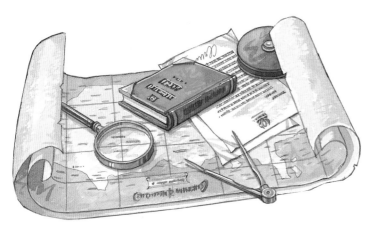

Limpet A type of mollusk, with a shell and a muscular foot, that clings to rocks in the sea.

Omen A happening or object believed to signal good or evil in the future.

Pack ice Large pieces of floating ice wedged together.

Rations A person's individual allowance of food and other supplies when there are shortages.

Rigging The ropes and wires attached to a ship's masts and sails.

Scurvy A disease, common among early sailors and polar explorers, caused by a lack of vitamin C.

Sextant An instrument used by sailors to calculate their position at sea. It works by taking measurements of the position of the sun and stars.

Stowaway A person who hides on board a ship so that he can travel for free.

Uncharted Not shown on any map.

Whaler A whale hunter or whaling ship.

Index

The Ross Sea Party

Shackleton's plan to cross the continent of Antarctica involved two ships. The idea was that Shackleton's team would travel to the South Pole from the Weddell Sea, carrying enough supplies to last for most of their journey. Meanwhile, a second ship, the *Aurora*, would land on the shore of the Ross Sea. A party from the *Aurora* would approach the pole from the opposite direction, leaving supplies for Shackleton's team to use on the final stage of their journey.

Three members of the *Aurora* team died, including their leader, Captain Aeneas Mackintosh—but they did succeed in setting up the stores as planned. However, since Shackleton's team never reached the pole, the stores were not used.

Shackleton's Vessels

Three vessels associated with Shackleton survive, at least in part.

The *Discovery* was a specially designed Antarctic research ship built in Dundee, Scotland. It was used for Captain Scott's Antarctic expedition of 1901–1904, on which Shackleton was third officer. Later, the ship was moored on the Thames in London for many years. It is now back in Dundee, and is open to the public.

The *James Caird*, the wooden lifeboat in which Shackleton sailed to South Georgia, is preserved at Shackleton's old school, Dulwich College, in London.

The Chilean Navy tugboat *Yelcho* was used by Shackleton in his rescue of the crew stranded on Elephant Island. The bow of the *Yelcho* is preserved at Puerto Williams naval base, in Chile.

Top Antarctic Explorers

Roald Amundsen (1872–1928)
The Norwegian Amundsen led the first successful expedition to the South Pole, arriving on December 14, 1911. He sailed on the *Fram* (which means "Forward"), built for an earlier Arctic expedition led by Fridtjof Nansen. In 1926, Amundsen and Oscar Wisting flew over the North Pole in the airship *Norge* ("Norway"), becoming the first people ever to visit both poles.

Amundsen's expeditions were very efficiently organized. Like the Inuit (the native people of the Arctic), he used dogsleds and wore warm but lightweight clothing made of animal skins.

Robert Falcon Scott (1868–1912)
Scott, an officer in the Royal Navy, led the *Discovery* expedition of 1901–1904, on which Shackleton also served. On the *Terra Nova* expedition of 1910–1913, Scott and four others reached the South Pole on January 17, 1912, only to find that Amundsen had arrived there first. All five of Scott's team died on the return journey.

Scott's team pulled their sleds themselves. The expedition had few dogs, and the ponies and motor vehicles they had brought with them could not withstand the conditions. Their woollen clothing was heavy and difficult to keep dry.

Shortly before his death, Scott wrote: "Had we lived, I should have had a tale to tell of the hardihood, endurance, and courage of my companions which would have stirred the heart of every Englishman."